Project Management Insti

D0836817

PLANNING IN
140 TWEETS

Quick tips on ideas, concepts, and the use of project
management in your profession and life

 @rvvargas

PLANNING IN
140 TWEETS

Quick tips on ideas, concepts, and the use of project
management in your profession and life

@rvvargas

Translation: Wagner Maxsen de Oliveira
Interior Layout: Sérgio Alves Lima Jardim
Cover Design: Sérgio Alves Lima Jardim

Library of Congress Cataloging-in-Publication Data

Vargas, Ricardo Viana.
[Planejamento em 140 tweets. English]
Planning in 140 tweets : quick tips on ideas, concepts, and the use of project management in your profession and life / Ricard Vargas.
    pages cm
Translation of the author's Planejamento em 140 tweets.
Includes index.
ISBN 978-1-62825-016-9 (English translation : alk. paper) -- ISBN 1-62825-016-X (English translation : alk. paper) -- ISBN 978-8574525716 (Portuguese version : alk. paper) 1. Project management. I. Project Management Institute. II. Title. III. Title: Planning in one hundred forty tweets.
HD69.P75V366 2013
658.4'04--dc23

                        2013032054

ISBN: 978-1-62825-016-9

Published by: Project Management Institute, Inc.
                14 Campus Boulevard
                Newtown Square, Pennsylvania 19073-3299 USA
                Phone: +610-356-4600
                Fax: +610-356-4647
                Email: customercare@pmi.org
                Internet: www.PMI.org

PMI Publications welcomes corrections and comments on its books. Please feel free to send comments on typographical, formatting, or other errors. Simply make a copy of the relevant page of the book, mark the error, and send it to: Book Editor, PMI Publications, 14 Campus Boulevard, Newtown Square, PA 19073-3299 USA.

To inquire about discounts for resale or educational purposes, please contact the PMI Book Service Center.

                PMI Book Service Center
                P.O. Box 932683, Atlanta, GA 31193-2683 USA
                Phone: 1-866-276-4764 (within the U.S. or
                Canada) or +1-770-280-4129 (globally)
                Fax: +1-770-280-4113
                Email: info@bookorders.pmi.org

One of the most spectacular project management teachers I have ever had the opportunity and happiness to meet.

During our last chat, he said: "Ricardo, you have to write a book that talks about projects in homeopathic doses, like tweets. People need to understand projects in a simple, practical, and direct way".

Well, here's the book!

THE AUTHOR

Ricardo Viana Vargas is a project, portfolio, and risk management specialist. During the past 15 years, he has been responsible for over 80 major projects in various countries in the petroleum, energy, infrastructure, telecommunications, information technology, and finance industries, comprising an investment portfolio of over 18 billion dollars.

He is currently the director of the Project Management Practice Group at UNOPS and lives in Copenhagen, Denmark. His work is focused on improving the management of humanitarian, peace-building and infrastructure development projects in dozens of countries, including Haiti, Afghanistan, Iraq, and South Sudan.

He was the first Latin American volunteer to be elected Chairman of the Board for the Project Management Institute (PMI), the largest project management organization in the world with more than 600,000 members, certification and credential holders, and volunteers in nearly every country in the world.

Ricardo Vargas has written eleven books on project management, published in Brazilian Portuguese and English, which have sold over 250,000 copies throughout the world.

In 2005 he received the PMI Distinguished Award and in 2011 the PMI Information Systems Community of Practice Professional Development Award for his contribution to the development of project management. He also received the PMI Professional Development Product of the Year award for the PMDome® workshop, considered the best project management training solution in the world.

He is a project management professor for various MBA courses, and actively participates on editorial boards for specialized journals in Brazil and the United States. Vargas is a recognized reviewer of *A Guide to the Project Management Body of Knowledge (PMBOK® Guide)*, the most important reference in the world for project management, and also chaired the official translation of the *PMBOK® Guide* into Brazilian Portuguese.

He is a chemical engineer and holds a master's degree in Industrial Engineering from UFMG (Federal University of Minas Gerais). Ricardo Vargas also holds a Master Certificate in Project Management from George Washington University and is certified as a Project Management Professional (PMP®), Risk Management Professional (PMI-RMP®), and Scheduling Professional (PMI-SP®) by PMI.

He is also certified as a PRINCE2® Practitioner

by the United Kingdom Office of Government and Commerce (OGC) and as Certified Scrum Master (CSM) by the Scrum Alliance. He attended the Program on Negotiation for Executives at Harvard Law School and has an executive formation in Strategy and Innovation from Massachusetts Institute of Technology (MIT).

Over an eleven-year time frame, which began in 1995, Ricardo, in conjunction with two partners, established one of the most solid Brazilian businesses in technology, project management, and outsourcing industries, which had a staff of 4,000 collaborators and an annual income of 50 million dollars in 2006, when Ricardo Vargas sold his share of the company to dedicate himself on a full-time basis to the internationalization of his project management activities.

He is a member of the Association for Advancement of Cost Engineering (AACE), the American Management Association (AMA), the International Project Management Association (IPMA), the Institute for Global Ethics, and the Professional Risk Management International Association (PRMIA).

www.ricardo-vargas.com

@rvvargas

facebook.com/ricardo.viana.vargas

linkedin.com/in/ricardovargas

DISCLAIMER

PRESENTATION

When I conceived of this book, the main idea was to create something for the general public, where the main concepts behind the activities of project planning and control would be presented in a simple, quick and direct way, and, for that, I borrowed the term "tweets."

As everybody knows, the microblog Twitter® has the objective of sharing ideas and information using up to 140 characters. I wasn't that rigorous in using this concept. You will certainly notice that some of the "tweets" go beyond this limit as I tried to convey the concepts in the best possible way.

The main target audience of this book is not the professional who has project management as his or her career. For these professionals I have 10 other books and more than 20 technical papers where I discuss the most important concepts and tools regarding project, program and portfolio management in a most detailed possible manner. The target audience for this book is the professional from other areas who wishes to have a preliminary knowledge of the subject and who also thinks that project management might contribute as a life skill, just like math.

This book is meant to be read by the lawyer, doctor, entrepreneur, researcher, public servant, and all other professions. Whatever your profession, every time that a temporary nature shows up in a work of yours, which is different from routine, you have in front of you a project. And managing a project is different than managing a routine.

In spite of being organized into themes, "Planning in 140 Tweets" does not have a classic reading sequence. You can just open the book on any page and read it. It doesn't have to be from the beginning until the end, theme by theme. What matters is the idea and the contemplation about each one of the small messages. It might be that one of them makes a big difference in your job or life, who knows?

Ricardo Vargas

TABLE OF CONTENTS_____

CHAPTER 1
BASIC CONCEPTS

Grasp the basic concepts related to project management and understand why so many people can't make a clear distinction between what is and what is not a project.

Since project management is a subject that is widely current, thus catching the attention of many people, professionals have been considering everything that they do as "projects." I have heard many people talking about the management of a project, such as "running the monthly payroll of an organization," or many other similar claims.

When talking about a project, we have to consider something that has its own unique characteristics. Projects are temporary events, which means that they have a start date, a period during which they are executed, and an end date. They are quite the opposite from a routine, which does not have a definite end, and that exists only when there is an interest to continue its existence.

The second characteristic that projects bear with them is to create unique products and services. These products and services have specific characteristics that differentiate them from the rest. It is as if each project has its own unique DNA. This characteristic turns projects into work environments with much more volatility and proneness to risks, when compared to traditional work.

Always bear in mind: *"A lot of the things that we currently do are projects. However, not everything is a project."*

01

The best way to understand what a project is is to compare it to routines. Project is everything that cannot be learned through repetition.

ROUTINE

The basic difference between routine
and projects. Routine: repetition
improves results. Project: innovation and
differentiated management improve
results.

Projects are temporary and unique.
Temporary because they respect a time
constraint. Unique because they have some
characteristics that set them aside from
everything that you've already done before.

Being temporary does not mean that the project is to be managed in a fast manner. There can be projects that last 1 day, 1 year, or even 10 years. What really matters is to ensure that there is an end.

04

There are 12 US$ trillion being invested in projects right now. This represents about 25% of the world's economy, with the involvement of more than 20 million professionals in project activities.
Source: Economist Intelligence Unit

05   STATISTICS

When planned, a project has much more chances to achieve the expected results. PMI states that low-performing projects endanger 27% of the budget. On the other hand, high-performing projects reduce the risk exposure to 3%.
Source: PMI Fact Book 2012

SUCCESS, PMI, STATISTICS   06

There is no such thing as perfection. A well managed project does not imply a perfect project. Mistakes and problems will most certainly happen. What is expected is that they will be minimized.

🖋 SUCCESS   07

Managing projects is about applying adequate knowledge and techniques so that the project bears more chances of success. Of course, it is you who decide whether to manage or just 'follow' the project from a distance!

08   SUCCESS 🖋

My favorite quote: **"Done is better than perfect!"**

Facebook - Palo Alto, CA, USA 🖋

🖋 QUOTE   09

The further in the future is any given work, the harder and riskier it is to manage.

TIPS, RISKS   10

Controlling a project is different from monitoring it. Control requires proactivity and involvement. Monitoring is just a passive task of observation.

11   CONTROL, SUCCESS, PROACTIVITY

What enables project success is its control, not just its monitoring.

CONTROL   12

In order for your project to fail miserably, you don't need to do anything. It will fail by itself. What requires effort and energy is the act of making sure it accomplishes its objective and follows the desired plan!

13

What ensures the success or failure of a project is the relationship between the scope of the work to be done, the available time, and the associated costs. These comprise what is known as **triple constraint.**

When we talk about success, we are obviously talking about the **execution** of the idea. Without a sound *business case* it's irrelevant to execute the project tasks well… The product will be strategically worthless.

BUSINESS CASE, SUCCESS 15

The organizational structure has a direct influence over the project work. The more rigid and departmentalized the organization is, the more challenging the projects will be.

16 TIPS

Be humble, don't overvalue your own project. Your project is not more important than the organization or the political and social environments inside which we all are.

TIPS 17

Many organizations use matrix structures to organize the aspects of their projects and routines. It can be a solution… but it has to be a temporary structure. The collateral effects and the conflicts will always be huge.

ROUTINE   (18)

Setting up a project management office (PMO) is definitely not the first thing to do when starting to work with projects. First, one has to learn about the subject, promote it internally and socialize the idea across the organization before taking bigger steps.

(19)   PMO *

And, finally, my favorite quote about executive support to planning: *"Executives never have time to plan… but there's always money to redo things all over again."*

QUOTE   (20)

CHAPTER 2
PROJECT MANAGEMENT AS A LIFE SKILL

One of my concerns is that I've seen a lot of people with the idea that project management is only for those who have chosen it as their profession.

And one of the biggest objectives of this book and specially the next tweets, is to show that several other professions can benefit from the concepts of project management.

The best correlation I can come up with is to compare project management to math. The basic concepts in math don't serve a purpose for a mathematician only. They are also valuable to an anthropologist, a lawyer, a language teacher. It's what I call the **concept of universal applicability**.

Within this same line of thought, many tools and concepts from the project management field can also be applied in many and diverse professions and personal activities.

How about taking advantage of the basic budgetary concepts to plan your next house renovation? What if the destiny of your next vacation trip could be chosen using portfolio and project selection tools? Those could be a very effective way to consolidate the wishes of your son or daughter, girlfriend or boyfriend, wife or husband, or even your own!

21

You don't have to build an atomic power plant to use project management. The concepts used in projects are also valid for your life, and not only for those professionals who work in the field.

Do not get caught by the misconception that says that project management is only for "big things." The concepts and tools are valid for all projects, including that tiny project that is inside your drawer.

22

You may even use *Post-It*® notes to specify your next vacation trip in detail and make sure that you are not leaving behind any work to be done.

23   WBS, SCOPE 🔖

During a family meeting, you can quickly discuss about the risks involved in remodeling your house and put them on paper. The simple fact of knowing about the existence of a risk already diminishes its exposure.

🔖 RISKS   24

If you are a lawyer, each one of your client's legal proceedings can be a project with a defined scope, objective, schedule, etc.

✎ SCOPE   25

You can use portfolio management tools to decide whether it is more advantageous to buy a car, go on a holiday trip, or remodel your house.

26   PORTFOLIO MANAGEMENT ✎

A doctor may use decision techniques and risk assessment tools to decide on the best approach to a given patient.

✎ RISKS   27

We must understand that knowing how to manage projects is like having an additional tool in our Swiss-made penknife. It is indispensable in a world more and more prone to projects and less prone to routines.

CHAPTER 3
THE PROJECT MANAGER

Get to know better the locomotive behind the project. In the next tweets, you will know the job of a project manager, his or her essential skills, and the scope of his or her work.

You will understand that the project manager plays the role of an orchestra conductor, the one who uses planning and leadership skills to transform ideas into results.

As you are probably imagining, there is a perception, though not always true, that the project manager must have a deep knowledge about the project technicalities. It may come as a surprise to you, but there are several studies that, when evaluating project successes and failures, have not associated project success with technical expertise.

It would be like affirming that a soccer coach must necessarily have had a brilliant career as a soccer player. What counts is knowing how to team the right group of people and train and inspire them toward a superior result.

In the project management world, it's basically the same thing. All you have to do is change the tactics and the championship trophy for the project and its result.

The project manager is ultimately responsible for project success. He or she monitors and supervises the results, besides leading the core project team.

LEADERSHIP

The project manager must, whenever possible, be chosen at the beginning of the project, ideally being present until the project close-out.

30

Basic characteristics of a successful project manager: generalist (able to understand the project context), excellent communicator and with great political awareness.

31   SUCCESS

The best technician is not necessarily the best project manager. Managing projects involves several other aspects, besides the technical expertise.

CREATIVITY, LEADERSHIP   32

Selecting a project manager is something that requires effort and dedication from the sponsor(s). It is undoubtedly the most strategic role in the project.

SPONSOR   33

Responsibility must walk hand in hand with authority. Don't expect distinguished results from a project manager if you don't grant him or her the adequate authority to lead the project.

34   AUTHORITY, LEADERSHIP

Who really manages the project is the project manager and his or her core project team. It is not an individual task: **it's a 100% team effort!**

TEAM   35

A mature project manager is someone who has already been exposed to several types of projects and performed different roles, without having necessarily any relationship with age or time in the organization.

One cannot guarantee that a professional who has experience in several areas of the organization will be a great project manager. Bear in mind that projects always represent something new and different.

When executing your job as a project manager, always have in mind the following phrase: *"If it were easy, anyone would do it."*

CHAPTER 4
A CAREER IN PROJECT MANAGEMENT

In this chapter I will discuss some of the points I believe to be fundamental for you to understand when deciding upon a career in project management.

There is a short-sighted perception from those who want to be project managers with respect to seeing only the benefits, the status, and the financial returns. A competent project manager can and should indeed receive worthy compensation. The problem lies therein, being competent.

In order to be a good project manager, one must have a set of competencies that go from an analytical planning prowess to entrepreneurship, from being able to perceive risks to leading people. It is not a set of extremely obvious skills that can be acquired very easily. Neither will an MBA nor a project management certification make you manage a project effectively.

The diploma and the certificate are important credentials, but the experience that you acquire every day and in every project is what turns you into a complete project manager, extremely sought after and valued.

As the world gets more and more "**projectized**," the project management career is clearly booming. But just like I don't sing or play soccer, being a project manager is not for everybody.

Life is cruel. As you get more experienced in project management, the opportunities get more challenging. Your financial compensation does not necessarily follow the same rule!

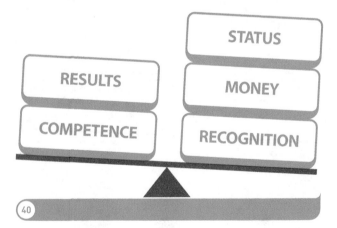

RESULTS

STATUS

MONEY

COMPETENCE

RECOGNITION

40

To be a project manager is to be a stress manager. Always have in mind that if somebody pays you to be a project manager, he or she is paying you to take charge of his or her stress and problems.

✎ CAREER 41

A good way to broaden your professional opportunities when it comes to projects is to be open to projects outside your area of expertise. Many of the concepts that pervade projects are universal and can be applied to different types of projects.

42 TIPS, CAREER ✎

Always start humble. Don't expect your first project to be a hydroelectric power plant. Maybe your next kitchen revamp or your next vacation trip would be an excellent starting point.

43

There is a huge market demand for
working with projects. The challenge, on
most occasions, is that the opportunities
are not always geographically where you
are. Be flexible about living in another
country!

44

The most popular certifications in project
management are, beyond the shadow
of a doubt, the **Project Management
Professional (PMP®)** credential from
Project Management Institute (PMI) and
PRINCE2® Practitioner from the Office of
Government Commerce (OGC).

45   CERTIFICATION, PMI, PRINCE2, CAREER

The project management certification
leverages the potential for opportunities to
at least getting the first job interview. What
secures the job for you is what you have
done with the knowledge you acquired in
previous projects.

CERTIFICATION, CAREER   46

CHAPTER 5
WHERE IT ALL BEGINS: THE BUSINESS CASE

One of the main causes for project failure happens when people start planning or executing the project without really knowing what is the result to be accomplished.

The **business case** is the compass that guides and reasons out the main benefits and justifications for the existence of a project.

The business case is not a document created just to make part of the documentation. It is a crucial evaluation of what you intend to do and what the benefits will be.

It usually includes:

- Feasibility study

- A background of how the project idea was born
- The project's main stakeholders
- Justifications, expected results, etc.

The business case is not limited to the above items, of course. It needs to be consistent enough to effectively support a decision on investing or not on a project.

One of the most common mistakes is to develop a business case only to justify a project that will be executed anyway. It would be like creating a business case to support a decision that had already been made! This is the opposite of how this process should be handled, which is to allow for dialogue and reasoning about the real need to implement the project.

And, contrary to what many people believe, it is equally beneficial when the final recommendation is to not execute the project, especially because you haven't spent much on the project yet. Can you imagine coming to the conclusion close to the final delivery date that it was not worth investing in the project ? That would be a catastrophe.

A project should only exist if there was a direct connection to solving a problem or leveraging an opportunity! Without a problem or an opportunity = no project!

Not knowing the reason why the project exists is the same as driving on a road without knowing exactly where you want to go.

SUCCESS   48

The *business case* should be the first document to be created in a project. It explains the fundamentals that justify the project's existence.

49   BUSINESS CASE

There is no rigid format to preparing a *business case*. A piece of paper with clear ideas from where to start and why you want to do something is per se an excellent first step.

SIMPLIFY, BUSINESS CASE   50

IDEA

BUSINESS CASE

IS FEASIBLE?

YES   NO

DISCARD

PLANNING

EXECUTION + CONTROLLING

RESULTS

The *business case* must approach several whys that need to be answered before starting any planning. It justifies the project's very existence.

🖌 BUSINESS CASE   51

The discussions about the reasons, problems, and benefits that need to be addressed by the *business case* should always be a team effort. This allows for the consideration and inclusion of different points of view.

52   TEAM 🖌

One should promote creativity and idea generation at the beginning of the project. If these arise during the final phases of project execution, especially when they have flamboyant characteristics, they are just nightmares.

🖌 CREATIVITY   53

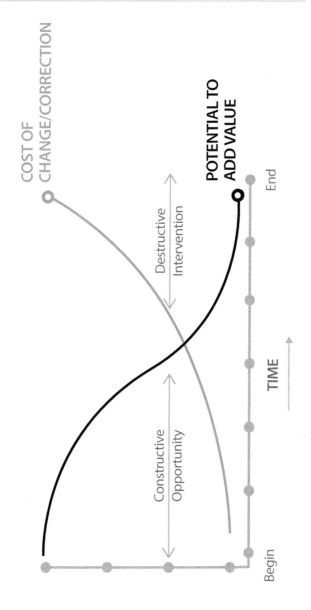

Always try to secure a sponsor for your work. He or she is your guarantee and necessary support to make the planning possible and, mainly, protect the project from the storms that may appear during project execution.

SPONSOR   54

CHAPTER 6
SIZING UP THE WORK TO BE DONE

In this chapter I will present the main aspects involved while preparing the project scope. Please remember that the objective here is not to actually plan the work, but to make sure that the product or service will be obtained using the least possible amount of effort.

This activity is extremely important and it is the base of all planning. It's about the eternal challenge of making more with less.

Some of the fundamental tools, like the work breakdown structure (WBS), will be presented and explained to demonstrate that the scope is nothing more than a detail, but clear and precise, of everything that must be done on the project, thus creating a solid base for the following planning activities, including determining the necessary schedule dates, costs, team, and risks.

When we adequately manage the project scope, we make sure the work to be done is clear and we also minimize the risks that usually arise from a distorted view of the desired products and services.

The first planning activity should be to define what the project will produce. If you don't know what has to be done, it's not possible to determine how long it will take and how much money will be needed to produce it!

COST, SCHEDULE, SCOPE, SUCCESS

The scope should clearly separate what will and what will not be done. It is like a frontier. If something is not defined as part of the scope, then it MUST be considered as out of the scope.

56

Scope is the project's DNA. It is impossible to know its risks or who will execute its tasks if we don't know anything about the required work.

57   QUOTE, RISKS

The WBS, or work breakdown structure, is the basic tool for project scope. It's like an organizational chart, but instead of roles and functions, it contains the project work divided into its necessary components.

WBS, SCOPE   58

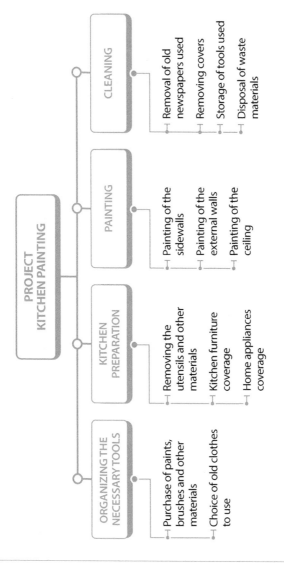

Example of a WBS

Each descending level of the WBS means an increase in the level of detail for the work to be done. The lowest level is usually known as a work package. It is inside this package that the work is actually executed.

WBS, WORK PACKAGE   59

The creation of a WBS allows for a better assignment of responsibilities and project costs, once each work cell is clearly specified.

60   WBS, RESPONSIBILITIES, COST

There are two classic ways to build a WBS: top-down, by using a decomposition technique, or bottom-up, through aggregation.

WBS   61

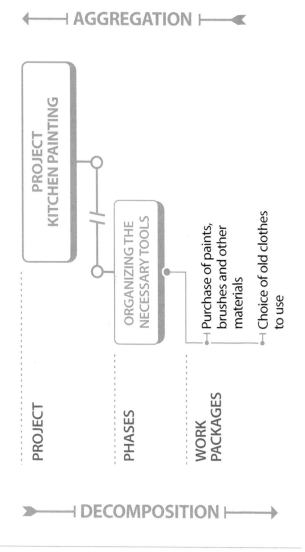

The two ways to build a WBS

When building a WBS using decomposition, one should start with the major phases of the project, which are then successively decomposed into smaller work groups until the desired level of detail is reached.

✏ WBS   62

The creation of the WBS using aggregation is more complex. It begins with a random generation of the work to be done and then these are grouped by similarities until you reach the project phases. It is like building up a Lego structure.

63   WBS ✏

If you have to choose just one document for your project, the WBS is the one. Believe me, it is more important than the schedule and the budget, for example.

✏ WBS, CONTROL, SCOPE   64

The only way to effectively assign responsibilities is through a clear and detailed definition of the project scope.

⚓ RESPONSIBILITIES   65

Two of the most indisputable evils regarding the scope of a project: Uncontrolled increase in scope *(Scope Creep)* and delivering more than planned *(Gold Plating)*.

66

The uncontrolled increase in scope happens when the already defined work starts to grow and incorporate even more work in a constant manner, thus damaging the deliveries. It is usually called the *Since We are Already Here Syndrome.*

67

Gold plating the work and products
represents adding a series of functionalities
that take time and use resources, but that
does not add value to the product.
If we gold-plate a metal, that does not turn
it into gold.

RESOURCES   68

Manage the scope or suffer the
consequences of the Porter Law: *"You will
always be asked to do more with less, until
you can do everything with nothing."*

69   QUOTE, SCOPE

CHAPTER 7
ESTABLISHING AND MONITORING DEADLINES

Project time management is perhaps the most visible planning activity. It is where we get the most benefits from software applications and other tools.

There is a problem with the excess of focus that people and organizations usually give to deadlines, trying to manage time in a desperate way. The truth is that time is not what really needs to be managed. Time is a consequence of the work to be done, of the risks that surround the project, and of the competence and motivation of the team, among other things.

What the organizations really have to do is to plan and manage other areas like scope, risks, and human resources in the best possible way so as to allow the results to be realized over time.

Whenever we say that a work is late, we have to immediately check what went wrong, where the problem was, and when it happened. Oftentimes, the real problem is hidden beneath the surface.

If you only manage the schedule and costs, it's like using a thermometer to find out a patient's disease. A schedule delay is an indicator of a problem, but not necessarily the problem itself.

COST

Determining the final end date in an arbitrary way, without considering the data and the required work is the same as dreaming at night and wanting that the dream come true on the following day.

✍ SUCCESS   71

A schedule is nothing more than a representation of the work to be done over time. It can be visually represented in various forms. Among the most popular ones are the Gantt Chart and the Network Diagram.

72   GANTT CHART, NETWORK DIAGRAM ✍

The Gantt Chart is the most popular way to represent a schedule. It is made of bars with a constant size placed on the calendar. Their length is directly proportional to their durations.

✍ GANTT CHART   73

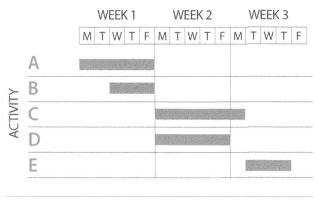

Gantt Chart

Another ofter used tool is the **Network Diagram**. It organizes the work in a logical sequence of execution.

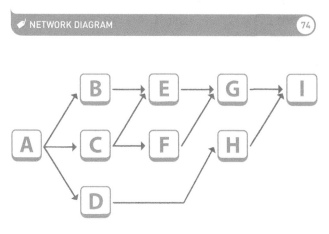

NETWORK DIAGRAM   74

A simplified example of a Network Diagram

In the network, the tasks are connected in a way that one task can only start after its predecessor has finished. This is called a Finish to Start relationship. There are other possible relationships, sucha as Start to Start, Finish to Finish, and even Start to Finish.

NETWORK DIAGRAM   75

Whenever possible, try to make all the relationships as Finish to Start. Don't make things more complicated creating complex relationships that will only upset you. Use them only when absolutely necessary.

76   NETWORK DIAGRAM, SIMPLIFY

You can always count on software to create your schedule (Microsoft Project, for example). But don't forget that a tool is always just a tool. The tool is never the project manager.

77

To be an expert in Microsoft Project without having project management skills is like being an expert in Microsoft Excel without knowing math. Dangerous!

QUOTE   78

A fundamental concept in any plan is the critical path. It is the path that contains all the work that, when late, causes the project to be late.

79   CRITICAL PATH

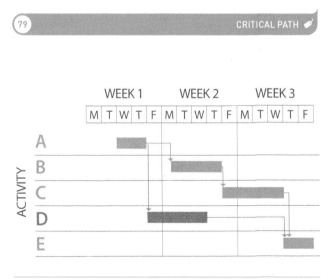

Gantt Chart showing the Critical Path (in blue)

The critical path can be calculated in a simple mathematical process, where the durations and potential start and finish dates of the tasks are assessed and their possible floats are identified.

🏷 CRITICAL PATH   80

The tasks that are scheduled with no float are those that most impact the project end date, and hence are called critical tasks.

81   CRITICAL PATH 🏷

The critical path relates exclusively to the project time period. It is not necessarily the **most expensive**, the **most technically challenging**, or the **most dangerous** project path.

82

Resources are all materials, equipment, and people that are used to perform the project work. They have a direct impact on the project duration.

RESOURCES   83

For the most part of the tasks, the amount of resources impacts directly on their durations. More people, less time. This is known as crashing.

84

It is very important to know that crashing mechanisms have a limited use; i.e., nine women together will not give birth to a child in only one month! This is known as the Law of the Diminishing Returns.

CRASHING, SCHEDULE   85

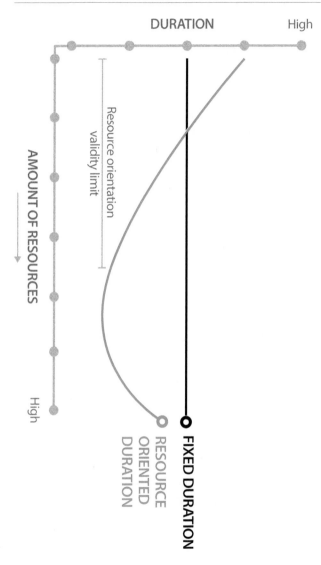

Exemplification of the Law of the Diminishing Returns

Crashing a project task means adding resources to it with the objective of reducing its duration. It is heavily used when the resource is relatively cheap when compared to the work to be performed.

CRASHING 86

One of the most traditional mechanisms to speed up the project is to execute more tasks in parallel. The biggest challenge to parallelism (or fast tracking) is to keep the risks below an accepted level of tolerance for the project.

87 RISKS, PARALLELISM

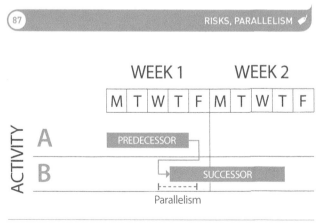

Applying parallelism (or fast tracking)

There is no use in executing non-critical tasks in parallel. If you do so, you're just increasing their float to the detriment of risks and quality.

🏷 PARALLELISM, RISKS   88

Don't forget: *"Planning is much more than managing time and creating schedules."*

89   QUOTE 🏷

CHAPTER 8
MANAGING COSTS AND BUDGETS

We can never be paranoid over costs. Before that, we may have to discuss the concept of value, which is related to the benefits that we wish to accomplish. Many times the challenge lies in transforming value into a a monetary currency, especially when the benefits are not clearly tangible. In this case, an additional effort is needed to question and try to clearly understand the value that each proposed benefit will bring to the project.

Just like time management, discussed in the previous chapter, cost is central to any project control. Everybody wants to make sure that the available budget is enough to deliver the expected benefits. It is important to note that cost is directly related to the work to be done and the available resources to do it.

Resources are materials, equipment, and people that are used to execute the project tasks. They basically consume the available money for the project.

Here's a hint: if what you are doing has no value, any cent spent on it is a fortune!

Cost is different from **price**. Cost is a function of the resources that you use in the project. Price is a business decision that is based on your competition and in the value perceived by the market.

The project cost is the sum of the costs for all resources that are required in the project, along with the respective administrative costs.

🖋 RESOURCES, COST   91

The most effective way to determine the project cost is by determining the costs of all work packages as defined in the work breakdown structure.

92   WBS 🖋

Human resources are compensated by taking into consideration their allocated time (hours, days, months). Materials are accounted for by their consumption and don't alter the costs if the task delays.

🖋 RESOURCES   93

The causes for budget overrun are related to the lack of clarity of the work to be done and also due to the inability to identify, assess, and respond to risks.

94   RISKS, SCOPE, SUCCESS 🖋

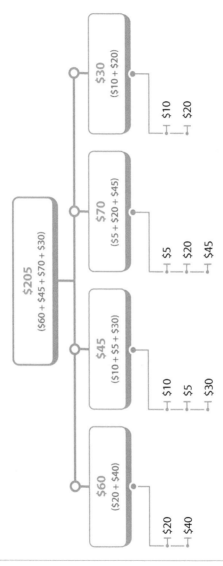

Cost estimate for work packages

Money is not a resource, but a resource cost. Money per se does not execute the work. What we use to perform the work is what costs money. Examples: mason, cement, paint, ladder.

95

Money would be a material if it were directly used in the work. Imagine wallpapering your bedroom with $100 bills. In this case, money (paper money) would be a material.

96

Controlling costs in an isolated way is a bad decision. The problems don't happen in the costs themselves, but impact them directly. That's why the project control must be done in an integrated manner.

CONTROL   97

CHAPTER 9
QUALITY MANAGEMENT

Quality is one of the most misunderstood concepts that I have ever seen. Oftentimes, behind a so-called justification for quality, we end up doing much more and also spending much more than originally planned. It may a spectacular feat to surprise and innovate when looked under the eyes of differentiation, but on the other hand, it can be very dangerous to do so when we do not grasp the exact meaning of benefit/cost for that quality, meaning what is and what is not worth doing.

The main concept behind quality with respect to planning and project management is that we have to focus on delivering the client needs. If we don't know what the client wants or needs, then we will most definitely have many difficulties in understanding what the quality for the product or service will be.

It is basically a management of expectations. And expectations can't be treated using simple math. Expectations are in fact molded by the cultural, social, and psychological aspects of each stakeholder. You don't have to deliver a product or service that looks just like you. You have to deliver something that looks just like your client.

I know for sure that what I have just said is not unanimously accepted. Steve Jobs was very blunt when he said he didn't take into consideration the need to research the client needs. He always said "...the consumer does not know what is good for him or her. We do!" Apple's current history clearly demonstrates that the products that were created under this model and 'speech' are extremely successful.

But this is an atypical case in an atypical company! It will certainly be a theme for discussion when our children and grandchildren read future economy books.

There is a direct connection between quality, cost, and benefits. Being the most expensive thing does not imply that it is the one with the best quality. Everything depends on the context and the objectives you may have.

BENEFIT, COST

Is a **Ferrari** better than a **VW Beetle**?
Oftentimes we think that what is expensive,
sophisticated, and luxurious is the one item
that bears the best quality. But if we want
a car to use on a farm with a dirt road, the
good and flexible VW Beetle might be an
option of much greater quality.

✎ COST   99

Quality means fulfilling the needs of the
client of the project. If you don't know what
your client's expectations are, it will be
impossible to know if what you are doing
will satisfy his or her needs.

100

Quality and scope walk side by side.
Oftentimes, the manner and the level of
detail by which the project is broken down
into work packages determine the quality
expectations for the project.

✎ WBS, SCOPE   101

PROPOSED BY THE SPONSOR

WHAT WAS PLANNED

WHAT WAS DELIVERED

WHAT THE CLIENT WANTED

A little bit of controversy: *"Surprising your client positively is not necessarily a good thing when we look at it under a planning perspective."* The cost and effort of the surprise can be seen as totally superfluous.

🖊 QUOTE   102

It's quite simple: *"Understand and deliver what your client wants. Do not deliver less than expected, but be careful with gold plating!"*

103   QUOTE 🖊

CHAPTER 10
LEADING PEOPLE

As we've already seen, to work with project management is always being between the frontiers of what is and what is not possible to do. That's why it is fundamental to have an impeccable team and leadership.

You have to imagine Mr. Edward A. Murphy, the famous guy who created a law that bears his own name, as one of your team members. He will always be there to tell you that "if something can go wrong, it will definitely go wrong."

Leading and inspiring the team towards a superior performance is one of the most critical tasks that the project manager and his or her team must accomplish.

We have to remember that what we have in front

of computers and machines are in fact people who have programmed them or just operate them, and these people are constantly under a level of great stress. Because of that, they need to be inspired and led in the most effective manner.

Leading a project means listening carefully to what the team, sponsor, client, and other stakeholders have to say, it is the only way to obtain a real understanding of everybody's needs.

104

Changing a project manager
during the advanced phases
of a project clearly opens
opportunities to undesired
changes in scope, thus increasing
the chances of failure.

RISKS, SCOPE

A base of power and leadership is built on integrity, constant example, and coherence in attitudes, but never on a hierarchical position or fear.

LEADERSHIP   105

In order for a project to succeed, the team members need to trust the professionals who lead the work.

106   SUCCESS, TEAM

Managing the stakeholders is as important as knowing the scope of what needs to be done. If you do not know who exerts a positive or negative influence on the work, you will not be capable of identifying all the risks that might happen.

SCOPE, STAKEHOLDERS, RISKS   107

Conflicts are part of the job. It is important to understand that not every conflict is bad and destructive. Oftentimes conflicts bring about change and new attitudes and perspectives to the team.

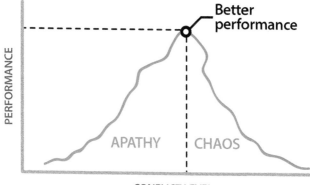

A team is a group of team with **diverse** skills, committed to a **common objective**. A soccer team would not be a team if there were 11 goalkeepers. Diversity makes the team.

TEAM   109

Here are some words that characterize a team: trust, respect, diversity, good relationships, critical sense, and common purpose.

110   TEAM

Do not think that the bigger the team is, the more powerful it will be. Many times a critical and complex project will not need too many people. Maybe all it needs is **really competent people**!

SUCCESS, TEAM   111

CHAPTER 11

UNDERSTANDING THE IMPORTANCE OF COMMUNICATION

When thinking about planning, one of the areas that we most improvise on is communication. More often than not, we consider the act of communicating as something natural and simple, but we end up not dedicating the right amount of time and effort to making sure the information flows effectively.

Communication is one of the areas most prone to different perceptions, cultures, and values. Oftentimes, simple gestures may be obvious to some, but they can be perceived totally differently by others.

Who hasn't ever experienced a situation where he or she was misinterpreted by somebody else?

In order to communicate in an effective way, it is very important to understand your audience and the message that is to be conveyed. We have to understand that a message to the president of the organization about a specific project is different than the message to be told to the project team, which is also different from the message to be distributed to the company in general.

This sounds strange, right?

Could I be possibly suggesting that you say something to a group of people, and another completely different thing to another group? Not at all. Please note that I said "message," not information. The message is the form that we use to encode the information. The information should be the same to all audiences. What changes is the approach that you use to formulate your message in a way that it makes the understanding easier for those who are about to receive it!

112

Communicating is much more than talking and hearing, writing and reading. Information and communication are the main supporters to every decision-making process.

Communication always has two sides: who gives information has to do it in a clear and direct way (sender). The one who receives it has to confirm that the message has been received and understood (receiver).

113

Remember: it is much easier to write a whole page than just one line. And, as Renato Russo, a Brazilian singer, once said: *"We should never say too much, when in fact we don't have anything to say."*

114   SIMPLIFY, QUOTE

Internal audience: project team, senior executives, other departments.
External audience: clients, providers, government, and the community. It is important to create messages that are specific to each audience!

115

Our current problem is not lack of information, but quite the opposite. This information overload pollutes and makes decision making much harder. Be clear, direct, and concise.

As we exited the elevator, we encounter the sign below.

What is the direction to room 102?

Data and information are two different things. **Data** is just something that has been collected but has no value all alone. Example: the task is 2 days late.

117

Information is the data after being processed, which later supports decision making. Example: the 2-day delay will bring about a $1,000,000 fine, thus causing the product to be commercially unachievable.

118

Everything that might distort the information and that doesn't belong to its content is considered to be a **noise** (or **interference**). Noises are created because of culture, values, emotions, judgments, and personalities.

TIPS   119

Every time somebody sends a message (be that a text, chart, or an oral comment during a meeting), he or she uses his or her own noises (culture, values, life experiences, judgments, and personality).

(120)

MESSAGE
SENT

NOISE

Noise is present in a process of encoding and decoding a message

When somebody receives a message, he or she decodes it according to his or her own noises. If the noises between who sends the information are different from the ones who receives that information, the risks of communication misinterpretation are evident.

121

CHAPTER 12

IDENTIFYING, ASSESSING, AND RESPONDING TO RISKS

In the next tweets I will discuss one of the areas that has received maybe more attention than others in the last couple of years: risk management.

The management of uncertainty has increasingly become more and more essential in everything we plan and do. We have to be sure that the plans we are developing are compatible with the risks we are willing to take.

In this case, the fundamental matter lies upon two basic things: **uncertainty** and **tolerance**. Uncertainty is what gives us the doubt about the inherent benefits and costs to do or not do something in order to avoid or leverage any given risk, which up to a period of time, exists only in our minds. Tolerance delimits how much loss we accept from a threat or even a gain from an opportunity.

Anyway, we must be aware that projects are usually riskier than routine. Projects are usually a relevant component of innovation, and that already puts them in a different level of risk when compared to business as usual. We have to be prepared for that. Whoever doesn't want to take risks, well, is not fit to work with projects!

122

"You want a valve that doesn't leak and you try everything possible to develop one. But the real world provides you with a leaky valve. You have to determine how much leaking you can tolerate."

Obituary of Arthur Rudolph - Saturn 5 Rocket Scientist ✎

You have to be careful, real life does not happen in **NTP** (Normal Temperature and Pressure) situations. Be prepared to adapt, change, and adjust your project to the different scenarios and risks.

TIPS   123

Risk management is a **PROACTIVE** task. Project success is dependent on the proactivity of the project team while anticipating unexpected events and coming up with ways to deal with them.

124   PROACTIVITY

The whole risk management process should be executed as a team effort, preferably a multidisciplinary one. This minimizes the impacts of the individual perceptions that might be extreme.

TEAM   125

Risks are events that may or may not occur, causing a positive or negative impact in the work to be done. Negative risks are usually known as **threats**, whereas positive risks are known as **opportunities**.

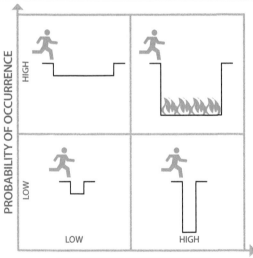

Risk profile for a person who wants to jump over a pit that has variable width and depth

Risk exposure is a direct function of the amount of money that is at stake when compared to the available resources. An exposure of $1,000 might be huge for some, but irrelevant to others.

127

The tolerance of organizations and people to a given risk influences its perception. Something that might be perceived as an extreme risk to some might be an irrelevant risk to others. The first step to understanding the risks is to understand the inherent tolerances.

128

Risk identification and analysis have a clear goal: to develop the possible responses that must be implemented. The classic responses to threats are: avoid, accept, mitigate, and transfer.

129

The main processes to manage risks are: **identify the risks**, **analyze the risks** (along with their probabilities of occurrence and impacts), **plan the risk responses,** and **monitor** them.

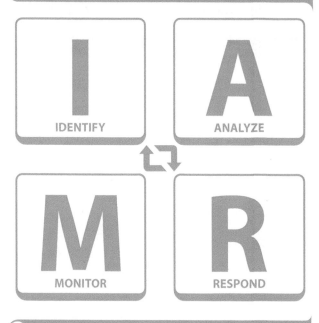

I
IDENTIFY

A
ANALYZE

M
MONITOR

R
RESPOND

Mitigate a risk means reducing its probability of occurrence and/or impact of its threat. Example: Install a new door lock in your home.

131

To **transfer** a risk means that we mitigate it by transferring its impact to a thirdparty. Example: to buy insurance for your car.

132

CHAPTER 13
PLANNING AND MANAGING CONTRACTS AND PURCHASES

This last chapter of the book deals with the third parties that provide products and services to the project, be those freelancers or other external suppliers.

The need for hiring external providers to execute part of the work or leverage the use of materials or equipment to make possible the execution of project activities is very common in many projects.

The first steps in this procurement process are focused on the make-or-buy decisions.

When we decide to do ourselves something that could be procured to external sources, this work becomes part of our project scope. But when we decide to obtain it from outside suppliers, the scope of work belongs to the external supplier and we play the role of clients for that particular scope. This decision is not always easy and it causes a direct impact on the project risks, budget, and deadlines. A detailed analysis must be made before making any decision.

As these external suppliers are not necessarily under our control, we must make certain they will be capable of delivering what has been agreed. The responsibility to deliver the project will always be ours, after all.

133

A decision that is always important during planning is to determine whether we will buy a product or service or produce it ourselves inside the organization.

SCOPE, RISKS

The decision to develop a product or service inside the executing organization needs to take into account a guarantee that the work is adequately included in the project scope.

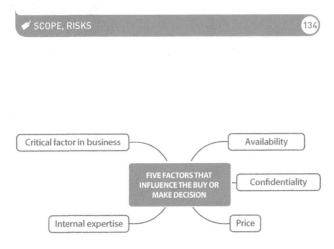

Critical factor in business

Availability

FIVE FACTORS THAT INFLUENCE THE BUY OR MAKE DECISION

Confidentiality

Internal expertise

Price

Availability, internal competence, price, confidentiality and expertise in the technology are among the **main factors** to be evaluated in a make-or-buy decision.

Elaborating a contract is not only a legal task, it is also used very often to minimize risks and make sure that the components of the plan will be fully delivered.

RISKS, CONTRACTS   136

The type of contract chosen for a provider has a direct influence on the associated risks for those who procure and those who sell the products and services.

137   RISKS, CONTRACTS

The more precise the scope of work, the more adequate it will be to use firm fixed-price contracts, since the job to be done is well known and can therefore be priced.

RISKS   138

On the other hand, the less precise the scope, the more adequate it will be to use cost reimbursement contracts. In this cases, a firm fixed price would incur a lot of additional costs for potential additional work, which represent a danger to the project.

RISKS, CONTRACTS, SCOPE   139

When procuring goods and services, pay attention to prices clearly below the market offer. Your joy will not last long.

140   QUOTE

GLOSSARY

Some definitions are based on the *PMBOK® Guide – Fifth Edition*.

Activity. A distinct, scheduled portion of work performed during the course of a project.

Assumption. A factor in the planning process that is considered to be true, real, or certain, without proof or demonstration.

Benchmarking. Benchmarking is the comparison of actual or planned practices, such as processes and operations, to those of comparable organizations to identify best practices, generate ideas for improvement, and provide a basis for measuring performance.

Brainstorming. A general data gathering and creativity technique that can be used to identify risks, ideas, or solutions to issues by using a group of team members or subject matter experts.

Business Case. A documented economic feasibility study used to establish validity of the benefits of a selected component lacking sufficient definition and that is used as a basis for the authorization of further project management activities.

Business Value. A concept that is unique to each organization and includes tangible and intangible elements. Through the effective use of project, program, and portfolio management disciplines, organizations will possess the ability to employ reliable, established processes to meet enterprise objectives and obtain greater business value from their investments.

Cause and Effect Diagram. A decomposition technique that helps trace an undesirable effect back to its root cause.

Constraint. A limiting factor that affects the execution of a project, program, portfolio, or process.

Crashing. A technique used to shorten the schedule duration for the least incremental cost by adding resources.

Critical Activity. Any activity on the critical path in a project schedule. Although some activities are "critical" in the literal sense, without being on the critical path, this meaning is rarely used in the context of projects.

Critical Path. The sequence of activities that represents the longest path through a project, which determines the shortest possible duration.

Critical Path Method. A method used to estimate the minimum project duration and determine the amount of scheduling flexibility on the logical network paths within the schedule model.

Decomposition. A technique used for dividing and subdividing the project scope and project deliverables into smaller, more manageable parts.

Duration. The total number of work periods (not including holidays or other nonworking periods) required to complete a schedule activity or work breakdown structure component. Usually expressed as workdays or workweeks. Sometimes incorrectly equated with elapsed time. Contrast with effort.

Effort. The number of labor units required to complete a schedule activity or work breakdown structure component, often expressed in hours, days, or weeks. Contrast with duration.

Fast Tracking. A schedule compression technique in which activities or phases normally done in sequence are performed in parallel for at least a portion of their duration.

Finish-to-Finish (FF). A logical relationship in which a successor activity cannot finish until a predecessor activity has finished.

Finish-to-Start (FS). A logical relationship in which a successor activity cannot start until a predecessor activity has finished.

Gantt Chart. A bar chart of schedule information where activities are listed on the vertical axis, dates are shown on the horizontal axis, and activity durations are shown as horizontal bars placed according to start and finish dates.

Milestone. A significant point or event in a project, program, or portfolio.

OGC. Created by the UK Government, the Office of Government Commerce (OGC) provided policy standards and guidance on best practice in procurement, projects, and estate management. It is now part of the new Efficiency and Reform Group within the Cabinet Office.

PMBOK®. The *PMBOK*® Guide contains the globally recognized standard and guide for the project management profession. It contains the fundamental practices that all project managers need to attain high standards and project excellence. This internationally recognized standard gives project managers the essential tools to practice project management and deliver organizational results.

PMI. PMI is one of the world's largest not-for-profit membership associations for the project management profession, with more than 700,000 members and certification and credential holders in nearly every country in the world.

PMP®. PMI's Project Management Professional (PMP®) credential is the most important industry-recognized certification for project managers. Globally recognized and demanded, the PMP® demonstrates that you have the experience, education, and competency to lead and direct projects.

Portfolio. Projects, programs, subportfolios, and operations managed as a group to achieve strategic objectives

Predecessor Activity. An activity that logically comes before a dependent activity in a schedule.

PRINCE2®. A process-based approach for project management, providing an easily tailored and scaleable project management methodology for the management of all types of projects. The method is the de-facto standard for project management in the United Kingdom and is practiced worldwide.

Product Scope. The features and functions that characterize a product, service, or result.

Program. A group of related projects, subprograms, and program activities managed in a coordinated way to obtain benefits not available from managing them individually.

Project Charter. A document issued by the project initiator or sponsor that formally authorizes the existence of a project and provides the project manager with the authority to apply organizational resources to project activities.

Project Management Office (PMO). An organizational structure that standardizes the project-related governance processes and facilitates the sharing of resources, methodologies, tools, and techniques.

Project Schedule Network Diagram. A graphical representation of the logical relationships among the project schedule activities.

Project Scope. The work performed to deliver a product, service, or result with the specified features and functions.

Quality. The degree to which a set of inherent characteristics fulfills requirements.

Residual Risk. A risk that remains after risk responses have been implemented.

Resource. Skilled human resources (specific disciplines either individually or in crews or teams), equipment, services, supplies, commodities, material, budgets, or funds.

Risk Breakdown Structure (RBS). A hierarchical representation of risks according to their risk categories.

Risk Mitigation. A risk response strategy whereby the project team acts to reduce the probability of occurrence or impact of a risk.

Risk Tolerance. The degree, amount, or volume of risk that an organization or individual will withstand.

Risk Transference. A risk response strategy whereby the

project team shifts the impact of a threat to a third party, together with ownership of the response.

Risk. An uncertain event or condition that, if it occurs, has a positive or negative effect on one or more project objectives.

Rolling Wave Planning. An iterative planning technique in which the work to be accomplished in the near term is planned in detail, while the work in the future is planned at a higher level.

Schedule Baseline. The approved version of a schedule model that can be changed only through formal change control procedures and is used as a basis for comparison to actual results.

Schedule Compression. Techniques used to shorten the schedule duration without reducing the project scope. See also Fast Tracking.

Scope Baseline. The approved version of a scope statement, work breakdown structure (WBS), and its associated WBS dictionary, that can be changed only through formal change control procedures and is used as a basis for comparison.

Scope Creep. The uncontrolled expansion to product or project scope without adjustments to time, cost, and resources.

Scope. The sum of the products, services, and results to be provided as a project. See also project scope and product scope.

Secondary Risk. A risk that arises as a direct result of implementing a risk response.

Sponsor. A person or group who provides resources and support for the project, program, or portfolio and is accountable for enabling success.

Stakeholder. An individual, group, or organization who may affect, be affected by, or perceive itself to be affected by a decision, activity, or outcome of a project.

Stakeholder Analysis. A technique of systematically gathering and analyzing quantitative and qualitative information to determine whose interests should be taken into account throughout the project.

Start-to-Finish (SF). A logical relationship in which a successor activity cannot finish until a predecessor activity has started.

Start-to-Start (SS). A logical relationship in which a successor activity cannot start until a predecessor activity has started.

Successor Activity. A dependent activity that logically comes after another activity in a schedule.

WBS Dictionary. A document that provides detailed deliverable, activity, and scheduling information about each component in the work breakdown structure.

Work Breakdown Structure (WBS). A hierarchical decomposition of the total scope of work to be carried out by the project team to accomplish the project objectives and create the required deliverables.

Work Package. The work defined at the lowest level of the work breakdown structure for which cost and duration can be estimated and managed.

TAG INDEX